WORKING IN
SPORTS

by Darlene Sigda Ivy

12
STORY
LIBRARY

www.12StoryLibrary.com

12-Story Library is an imprint of Bookstaves and Press Room Editions

Produced for 12-Story Library by Red Line Editorial

Photographs ©: Tassii/iStockphoto, cover, 1; a katz/Shutterstock Images, 4; Leonard Zhukovsky/Shutterstock Images, 5; Joyce Boffert/Shutterstock Images, 6; Debby Wong/Shutterstock Images, 7; digitalskillet/iStockphoto, 8, 29; Microgen/Shutterstock Images, 9; James G CC2.0, 10; Aspen Photo/Shutterstock Images, 11, 25; Henrik Lehnerer/Shutterstock Images, 12; Laszlo Szirtesi/Shutterstock Images, 14, 28; Eric Broder Van Dyke/Shutterstock Images, 15; Eric Charbonneau/Invision/AP Images, 16; Helga Esteb/Shutterstock Images, 17; SpeedKingz/Shutterstock Images, 18; selimaksan/iStockphoto, 19; ESB Professional/Shutterstock Images, 20; Steve Debenport/iStockphoto, 21; Joe Ferrer/Shutterstock Images, 22; FlashStudio/Shutterstock Images, 23; Haslam Photography/Shutterstock Images, 24; lostinbids/iStockphoto, 26; Mark Herreid/Shutterstock Images, 27

Library of Congress Cataloging-in-Publication Data
Names: Ivy, Darlene Sigda, 1952- author.
Title: Working in sports / by Darlene Sigda Ivy.
Description: Mankato, Minnesota : 12 Story Library, 2018. | Series: Career
    files | Includes bibliographical references and index. | Audience: Grade 4 to 6.
Identifiers: LCCN 2016047458 (print) | LCCN 2016054182 (ebook) | ISBN
    9781632354495 (hardcover : alk. paper) | ISBN 9781632355164 (pbk. : alk.
    paper) | ISBN 9781621435686 (hosted e-book)
Subjects: LCSH: Sports--Vocational guidance--Juvenile literature. |
    Occupations--Juvenile literature.
Classification: LCC GV734.3 .I89 2018 (print) | LCC GV734.3 (ebook) | DDC
    796.023--dc23
LC record available at https://lccn.loc.gov/2016047458

Printed in the United States of America
022017

Access free, up-to-date content on this topic plus a full digital version of this book. Scan the QR code on page 31 or use your school's login at 12StoryLibrary.com.

Table of Contents

Athletes Dream Big

Athletes dream of winning a gold medal or scoring the winning run. Or maybe they hope to break a world record. But is that realistic?

In the United States, three of every four boys play sports. Two of every three girls play. That's about 28.7 million kids. But there are only about 13,700 professional athletes. These aren't great odds. Only 1 in 2,100 kids might become a pro.

Most sports require coordination and endurance. But that's not enough. Athletes must be in great shape. They must train, exercise, and eat carefully. Professional athletes

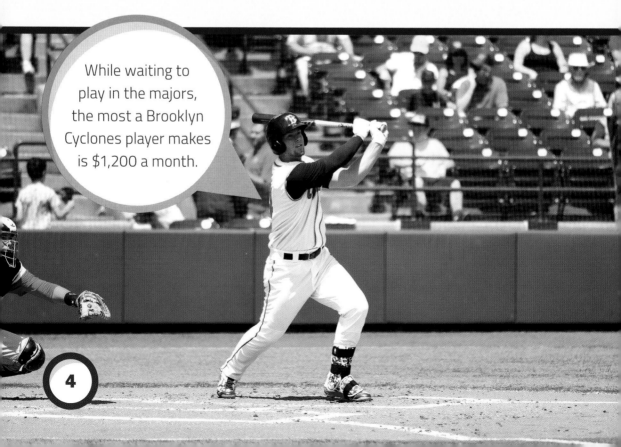

While waiting to play in the majors, the most a Brooklyn Cyclones player makes is $1,200 a month.

1

Number of female high school basketball players, out of 13,015, that turn pro.

- Many boys and girls play sports, but few go on to become professional athletes.
- Professional athletes have to practice for many hours.
- Many professional athletes don't earn a lot of money.

practice for hours. They may polish their skills in college.

Athletes work hard. Minor league baseball players work 60–70 hours a week during the season. They travel a lot. They have to work nights and weekends. And most earn as little as $1,100 a month. Few athletes earn million-dollar salaries. In 2015, the average salary for all athletes was $93,000.

FINDING A FOCUS

Some young athletes pick their sports early. Michael Phelps started swimming at seven. Simone Biles visited a gymnastics center at five or six. Others, such as Alex Morgan, try out different sports. She didn't focus on soccer until she was 14.

Simone Biles knew she wanted to be a gymnast from a very young age.

Coaching Is Key

A coach has to know each player's strengths and weaknesses. Coaches help players be their best. Coaches also help the players work as a team. They teach players new skills. Coaches encourage players who are in a slump. They plan the team's offense and defense for every game. They work long hours, nights, and holidays.

Many coaches are former players. In a recreational league, a parent may be the volunteer coach. In school sports, teachers who played sports may also be coaches. They learned the sport by playing. A new coach might start by working with young children or by being an assistant coach.

A professional head coach's job is always on the line. The team

Becky Hammon (right) played for the New York Liberty before becoming an assistant coach for the San Antonio Spurs.

Joe Girardi (right) has managed the New York Yankees since 2008.

must win. Most of these coaches learn by coaching college sports. Then they move to the pros. They might begin as assistant coaches, specializing in offense, defense, or a certain position. They might coach third base or the kicking squad. Some coaches prefer these specialized jobs. Others compete for the ultimate job of head coach.

$3,000
Maximum season's salary for half of all US high school basketball coaches.

- A coach helps team members play better.
- Coaches are often former athletes.
- Many professional coaches start by coaching one specific part of a sport.

SHORT-TERM JOB

Coaches for professional teams can earn million-dollar salaries. But they don't have job security. For example, 10 years is a long time to be a manager in Major League Baseball. Many coaches have been with their teams for less than five years.

Trainers Help Good Athletes Become Great

The people helping an injured athlete off the field are probably athletic trainers. Trainers care for athletes at sports events. They also help athletes recover from injuries. Trainers create exercise programs. These exercises help athletes strengthen muscles and prevent injuries.

Many trainers work for one professional team. Others work with a school and all its teams. And some work for just one athlete. Athletic trainers have to understand a variety of sports. Each sport requires a different set of skills. The trainer must plan exercise programs for different muscles.

Trainers also need good people skills. They work with athletes of all ages. And working with people who are injured can be difficult. It takes patience and understanding. Athletes may be upset about their injuries. Athletic trainers also work with medical professionals to help athletes stay healthy.

Trainers help athletes perfect their techniques.

A GROWING FIELD

Athletic trainers help people get fit and recover from injuries. Awareness of sports-related injuries is on the rise. This means more people are likely to seek the help of athletic trainers.

Many colleges offer programs to be an athletic trainer. It's important to understand how the human body works. Students study psychology, nutrition, kinesiology, and biology. Students also spend many hours in clinics. They practice skills and help injured athletes. After college, students take a test. Then they can work as a certified athletic trainer.

25,400
Number of athletic trainer jobs in the United States in 2014.

- Athletic trainers treat athletes with injuries. They also help athletes prevent injuries.
- Trainers work with coaches, athletes, and medical professionals.
- In college, students who want to be trainers study psychology, nutrition, and biology.

Some trainers create drills to help athletes get better.

Scouts Find New Talent

Every year, college athletes graduate. Every season, professional players retire. And every time, new players step up to take their places. A scout knows what players a team needs. It's the scout's job to find these talented athletes.

Scouts look for talented high school and college players. Scouts search newspapers and the Internet for information. High school and college coaches also tell scouts about special athletes. Scouts can watch videos of players. They can see if the players have the skills to succeed.

Scouts also travel a lot. They watch games in person. Scouts watch each player several times. They keep detailed records. Then they talk to athletes and their coaches. A scout needs to know the athlete wants to succeed and improve. And the athlete must

Some baseball scouts use radar guns such as this one to measure how fast pitchers can throw.

Football scouts often attend college games to look for talent.

have the personality to fit in with the team.

Scouting requires an excellent understanding of the sport. A college degree or playing experience isn't required. But many scouts have a bachelor's degree in sports management or business. Many scouts have also been athletes. Scouts often begin as a coach or a part-time scout. A scout gets promoted by finding good players.

$31,000
Average salary for a sports scout in 2014.

- College and professional teams need new players every year.
- Scouts research players to find a good fit for their team.
- Scouts look for players with good skills and a good attitude.

THINK ABOUT IT

Imagine you are a scout. In addition to athletic ability, successful athletes need the right attitude. Make a list of the qualities you would look for in a player.

Agents and General Managers Take Care of Business

Agents take care of the details. That way, athletes can focus on competing. But different agents have very different jobs. Some agents take care of only one player. They keep the player organized. They might negotiate contracts for the player. They hire trainers and other personnel support. And they work with the press for good publicity.

General managers keep an entire sports organization working well. They solve conflicts between owners and players. They work with marketing to get publicity and sell tickets. They manage the budget. Uniforms, equipment, and travel plans are their responsibility. They may also draft players and hire coaches and staff. Of course, managers have help.

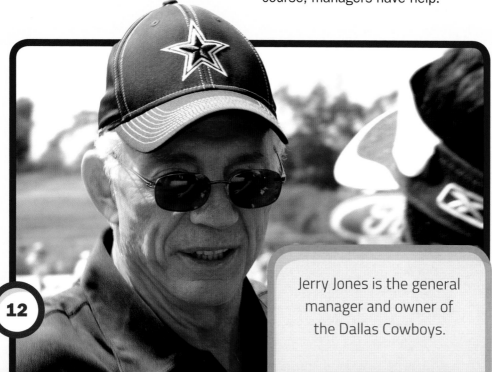

Jerry Jones is the general manager and owner of the Dallas Cowboys.

Large professional teams have assistant managers and office staff. Managers of college or amateur teams have less help.

Most managers are passionate about their sport and team. They like the idea of running a sports business. They want to create a winning team. That takes a lot of work and time. Sometimes managers travel with the team. Other times, they stay home to make deals. Managers feel a lot of pressure to win. If their team loses too much, managers can lose their jobs.

Many managers have a bachelor's degree in business or marketing. Some have advanced degrees in sports management or law. Many managers start out with a team as an intern. Others work with their college teams.

57
Number of coaches, scouts, training staff, and media relations staff for the Pittsburgh Penguins in 2016.

- A manager can work for one athlete or for a whole team.
- A team manager takes care of the business of sports, from ordering uniforms to hiring new players.
- Many managers study business or marketing in college.

Officials Enforce the Rules

Most sports have an official near the action. Officials keep competition safe, fair, and orderly. Officials work whenever athletes compete. That means working nights, weekends, and holidays.

Being an official can be stressful. Officials have to know the rules, even the ones that aren't well known. They make tough calls quickly. Sometimes players and coaches become upset over a ruling. But officials must stay calm. For everyone's safety, they can throw someone out of the game.

Soccer officials use yellow and red cards to enforce the rules.

68

Number of umpires in Major League Baseball each year.

- Officials help keep sports safe and fair.
- An official must know and apply the rules of the game.
- Officials need to watch each play while also staying out of the way of the action.

Many officials have to be in shape. They run up and down the field with the athletes. They have to know where the play is going. They need to dodge the action. But they must also see every play.

THINK ABOUT IT

Imagine you are an official in a game. People are angry about one of your calls. How would you stay calm in that situation?

Officials at recreational games are often volunteers. At higher levels, officials usually attend training and pass a test. Officials also improve their skills on the job. A professional sports official has years of experience and special training.

Major League Baseball has never had a female umpire as of 2016.

The Numbers Don't Lie

In 2002, Billy Beane was the general manager for the Oakland Athletics. The team's owners had given him a small budget to work with. Beane could not afford to sign well-known players. He turned to Paul DePodesta. DePodesta introduced Beane to a new way of using statistics to find undervalued players. Their plan worked, and the Oakland A's won the American League West Division that year. Their success has led many other professional teams to rethink the way they could use statistics, too.

Statisticians collect information. In sports, statisticians watch every play carefully. They record information. Who has the fastest time? Who has the most wins? Announcers love to share these details. And sports fans enjoy learning them.

But statisticians do more than collect trivia. Statisticians use information. They look at the numbers. They analyze and explain them. They try to find answers to questions. Who has fewer errors at first base? Which quarterback is better?

Beane (left) was played by Brad Pitt in *Moneyball*, a movie about Beane's use of statistics.

Is a swimmer faster on the first relay leg or the last? In sports, answers could help a team win.

Computers make collecting information easy. But it's hard to compare information. It may be even harder to explain the results. That is why statisticians need extra education. Statisticians earn a bachelor's degree in math or

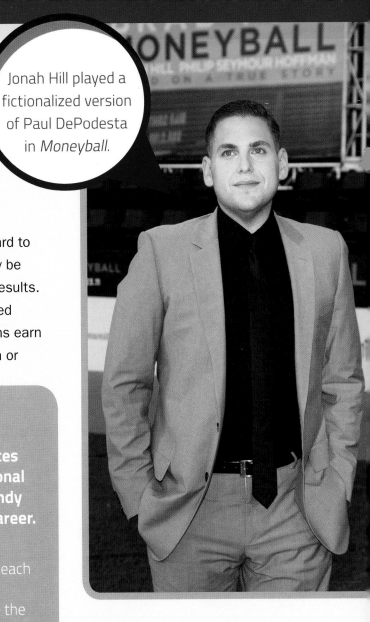

Jonah Hill played a fictionalized version of Paul DePodesta in *Moneyball*.

9,068

Total number of aces served by professional US tennis player Andy Roddick during his career.

- Sports statisticians record the details of each game.
- Statisticians analyze the data to answer questions about how athletes and teams can be more competitive.
- Statisticians use computers to crunch numbers, but they have to be able to explain what those numbers mean.

statistics. Many jobs also require a master's degree. Statisticians write computer programs, too. Programs analyze the information and create useful results.

Sports Doctors Help Injured Athletes Bounce Back

Sports headlines are often filled with stories of injuries. When athletes practice or play, they risk being injured. Some doctors specialize in sports medicine. They work with athletes of all ages and skill levels. Sports doctors help people find a healthy lifestyle. They promote lifelong fitness without illness and injury. Sports doctors can help anyone trying to stay fit.

They work with other doctors, trainers, coaches, and therapists. Sports doctors suggest fitness programs. They plan strength training and conditioning. To improve performance, they suggest changes in diet.

Sports doctors also work with injured athletes. A sports doctor can decide

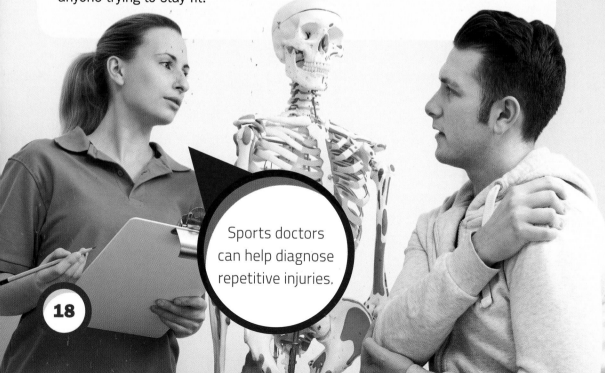

Sports doctors can help diagnose repetitive injuries.

18

90

Percentage of sports injuries that do not require surgery.

- Some doctors specialize in helping athletes stay fit and recover from injuries.
- A sports doctor may work for a team or with players in just one sport.
- Sports doctors work with coaches, trainers, and therapists to help an athlete.

when a sick or injured athlete is ready to play again.

Some sports physicians specialize even more. For example, they might work for one sports team. Or maybe they treat only tennis players. But other sports physicians work independently. They usually work regular clinic hours. They must be available for emergencies, too.

Sports physicians are like all doctors. They must be kind and patient. They need to communicate well. They must enjoy science. Training to become a sports doctor starts with four years of college. Students then take four years of medical school. That is followed by three to seven years of internships and residencies in sports injuries and treatment. Then the doctor also takes an exam to be certified as a sports medicine specialist.

Sports teams work with orthopedic surgeons who can repair many parts of the body, including the spine.

19

Anyone Can Help Others Get Moving

It's easy to get moving. Age does not matter. Camps, parks, community centers, and gyms are all great places to get active.

Recreation workers supervise fun activities. It may be a simple game of tag. It could be a silly version of balloon soccer. It could be a yoga or dance class. Workers organize practices for new sports skills. The program may be part of a

recreational league. These have teams that play against one another.

Recreation workers need to be physically fit. They need lots of energy and patience. Some workers teach many things. They might teach the basic skills and rules of several sports. They need to show good sportsmanship and teamwork, too.

Recreation workers often work in after-school or community programs. Many start by volunteering with younger children. They learn to work

Many community centers offer yoga classes.

20

$23,320

Average salary for US recreation workers in 2015.

- Recreational workers work with people of all ages in a variety of community settings.
- Recreational workers organize activities to help people stay active and healthy.
- Many workers work after school or during evenings and weekends.

with groups on the job. Recreation workers typically need at least a high school diploma. Some workers also have a college degree in recreation, physical education, or education.

Recreation workers often work evenings and weekends. Summer and vacation camps need recreation workers, too. Many recreation worker jobs are part time. But this work offers many opportunities to be fit and healthy.

Some recreation workers are referees for youth soccer games.

The Media Captures All the Action

People in the United States love sports. And they pay a lot of attention to sports reporters. These reporters give fans the play-by-play descriptions. They also highlight dramatic plays.

Sports reporters explain what is happening in the game. They make it interesting for people who are not there in person. Sports photographers capture images of great plays. Sports camera crews record the action on video. All these people work in journalism. Television, radio, and newspapers need sports news. Job opportunities increase each year. But sports reporters must be prepared to work nights, weekends, and holidays.

Many sports reporters begin with on-the-job training. One way for students to gain experience is by reporting on their school's sports. They can post pictures and comments on social media. Local television stations looking for news from the game

A reporter interviews pro cyclist Megan Guarnier

Sports photographers use large lenses to get close to the action.

can find these messages. If the comments are good, the student reporter might be asked for more. Many professional reporters have a bachelor's degree in communication. Many also played sports in college. They worked on the college newspaper, too. Some completed internships for a newspaper or television station.

127,000

Number of hours of sports on broadcast and cable television in all of 2015.

- Sports reporters help fans enjoy sports.
- Photographs, videos, and written sports stories share information about sporting events.
- Aspiring sports reporters can gain experience by posting informative social media comments about a game.

SPORTS ON TELEVISION

Five of the top ten broadcast and cable television programs of 2015 were football related.

1. Super Bowl XLIX: New England vs. Seattle
2. Super Bowl Post-Game
3. AFC Championship: Indianapolis vs. New England
4. College Football Championship: Ohio State vs. Oregon
9. NFL Playoff: Baltimore vs. New England

Psychologists Think like a Winner

There are many great athletes. But not every great athlete wins. Sometimes great athletes get nervous and lose. Maybe they can't focus on the game or the race. Coaches help athletes prepare physically. Sport psychologists help athletes prepare mentally. They help athletes think differently. The athletes then compete more successfully.

Sometimes athletes no longer want to train or compete. Sport psychologists can help make sports fun again. When athletes compete, they are under a lot of pressure. Coaches, parents, and even the athletes themselves expect to win. Sport psychologists help athletes handle this stress. Psychologists can help athletes develop pep talks.

The athletes talk to themselves before competing. Psychologists can also help athletes see success

Snowboarder Jamie Anderson used meditation when competing at the 2014 Winter Olympics.

6

Number of full-time sport psychologists at the US Olympic Training Center.

- Even great athletes need help to mentally prepare for competition.
- Sport psychologists help athletes cope with the pressure to win.
- Many college and professional teams have a sport psychologist on staff.

in their minds. This process is called visualization. For example, a track runner might imagine herself clearing every hurdle. This helps the athlete relax and become more confident. Then it is easier to jump over the hurdles.

Sport psychologists usually work in a private office. But they can also work for college or pro teams. They meet with athletes in an office or at the sports arena. Sport psychologists have to earn a bachelor's degree and also a master's degree in counseling.

Many athletes want help to improve and win. Sport psychologists can give athletes something extra. As sports become more competitive, sport psychologists may be more in demand.

Track athletes sometimes picture themselves clearing hurdles before a big race.

Athletes Eat to Fuel Their Bodies

Before every speed skating race, Bonnie Blair ate a peanut butter and jelly sandwich. It gave her the energy she needed to be fast. And Blair wasn't just an ordinary speed skater. She is the best US female speed skater ever.

Blair figured out what food her body needed. A sports nutritionist can suggest the best foods to eat for peak physical performance. Food is fuel for the body. Sports nutritionists learn what fuel the

body needs for each sport. The body also needs different food for training, competing, and recovering. Nutritionists suggest what athletes need to eat and when. They also help athletes plan food for hectic travel schedules. They help athletes perform well and stay healthy.

Nutritionists must enjoy science. They must also communicate well. Planning precise diets also requires attention to detail. Sports nutritionists must keep track of the

Nutritionists help athletes figure out their meals.

Some cross country runners eat lots of pasta the night before a race.

drugs and foods athletes cannot have. Taking some substances can disqualify an athlete. Many steroids are banned by professional sports organizations.

Some sports nutritionists begin with a few months of special training. But most have a bachelor's degree in nutrition. Many also have a master's degree and special training to work with athletes. Most states require nutritionists to take an exam and be certified. Some sports nutritionists work at colleges and universities or athletic clubs. Others work for food corporations or rehabilitation centers.

2,224

Estimated number of calories a 130-pound (59-kg) runner burns when running a marathon.

- Sports nutritionists understand how the human body uses food to make energy.
- When athletes eat the right foods, they can compete more successfully.
- Nutritionists recommend athletes eat different foods for training, competition, and recovery.

Other Jobs to Consider

Massage Therapist

Description: Relieve pain for athletes and help them heal from injuries

Training/Education: Licensure or certification, depending on the state

Outlook: On the rise

Average salary: $38,040

Sports Facilities Maintenance Worker

Description: Maintain athletic fields, tracks, golf courses, or other sports facilities

Training/Education: No formal education needed

Outlook: Steady

Average salary: $25,500

Sports Lawyer

Description: Provide legal representation for players, coaches, officials, administrators, schools, and facility owners
Training/Education: Law degree and passage of a state's written bar examination
Outlook: Steady
Average salary: $115,820

Sports Marketing Manager

Description: Create programs to advertise and promote sports teams or businesses
Training/Education: Bachelor's degree
Outlook: Steady
Average salary: $124,850

Glossary

ace
A serve in tennis that is not returned by the opponent.

biology
The study of life and living things.

conditioning
A regime of exercise, diet, and rest that helps an athlete become physically fit.

intern
A student or recent graduate who works for a certain time to gain experience.

journalism
The work of gathering news and images to be reported on television, radio, or in newspapers.

kinesiology
The study of the way humans move.

negotiate
To try to reach an agreement by discussing something.

official
An umpire, referee, or judge who is in charge during a sports event.

psychology
The study of the human mind and how it works.

publicity
Information about a person or event that appears in the media to gain people's attention.

recreational
Done for fun.

strength training
Exercise that uses weights to increase strength and build muscles.

visualization
The practice of imagining something.

For More Information

Books

Gerber, Larry. *Dream Jobs in Sports Refereeing*. New York: Rosen, 2015.

Mattern, Joanne. *So, You Want to Work in Sports?* New York: Aladdin, 2014.

Raymos, Rick. *STEM Jobs in Sports*. Vero Beach, FL: Rourke, 2014.

Visit 12StoryLibrary.com

Scan the code or use your school's login at **12StoryLibrary.com** for recent updates about this topic and a full digital version of this book. Enjoy free access to:

- Digital ebook
- Breaking news updates
- Live content feeds
- Videos, interactive maps, and graphics
- Additional web resources

Note to educators: Visit 12StoryLibrary.com/register to sign up for free premium website access. Enjoy live content plus a full digital version of every 12-Story Library book you own for every student at your school.

Index

About the Author

Darlene Sigda Ivy grew up in western Massachusetts, listening to the summer sounds of the nearby minor league baseball stadium. She now lives in southern Maine and is still a big sports fan.